The Feather Boy

I0110725

By the Same Author

The Feather Boy
and other poems

Judith Rodriguez

PUNCHER & WATTMANN

© Judith Rodriguez 2018

This book is copyright. Apart from any fair dealing for the purposes of study and research, criticism, review or as otherwise permitted under the *Copyright Act*, no part may be reproduced by any process without written permission. Inquiries should be made to the publisher. Every effort has been made to secure permission to publish translations of the works by Colombian poets.

First published in 2018
Published by Puncher and Wattmann
PO Box 441
Glebe NSW 2037

http://www.puncherandwattmann.com
puncherandwattmann@bigpond.com

National Library of Australia
Cataloguing-in-Publication entry:
Rodriguez, Judith
The Feather Boy and other poems
ISBN 9781925780079
I. Title.
A821.3

Cover design by Miranda Douglas
Printed by Lightning Source International

Australian Government

Australia Council
for the Arts

This project has been assisted by the Australian Government through the Australia Council, its arts funding and advisory body.

Contents

The World We Live In

The Feather Boy

A feather caught in grass tells of the wind.
It must fill or fall. I am eight,
floating in the lane's dark flue, the feathers in my fist.

War takes me for a man. Up ahead is where
shots rattle like a knocked door
and break off. The men met where they said

are running, we run too, to a shout and its botching.
My knees catapult me
out from the wall's foot, and my dark charges

lie like spent shells, faces by barely daylight
light enough to find with hand
stretched, then (crouching) cupped from the stir of air—

light enough for the feathers I save to betray life.
I am the feather-boy. If I call,
a knife makes sure. And I call, for us crushed in hiding,

for all of us scattered, parents, cousins, our fates
feathers in war's updraft.
Next day in the yard, there's a farm hand with a message

or a stranger looking too long, strong as my brother,
a man to rot in the wood.
The forest feathers prickle and stoop in my pocket.

This poem is based on the account of a Holocaust survivor who was the eight-year-
old "feather boy" with a partisan group resisting the Nazi occupation.

Wallenburg

Hungary's first detailed account of the disappearance of the Swedish diplomat Mr Raoul Wallenburg in 1945 ... said he was unjustly jailed by the Soviets and died in a Moscow prison in 1947. News item, 1987

They know they must kill
Wallenburg, who all these years
shines, rotting in hell
somewhere in Siberia,

now forty cold years
of his identical face
clenched in wind, witness
the prisoners' amazement,

sightings, hopes, a name
war details cannot bury
nor our wreaths placate
nor our stones. He lives on less—

the saved speak,
the dead recount their ration,
jailers mince files,
the body disappears:

Wallenburg lives.

To Sleep, 1986

Then there's the bed-size morass
between the news and day.
No matter that there fluttered
a tender gathering of small clouds
high over the shredded plane-trees.
South Africa is burning awake
screaming in the obscene necklace
and the grave political sentences
char and the stench rams us
and the dying of Chernobyl reach out
in a claim to stand for generations.
Any dust serves the squall
of the unlearning human spirit.
Inhuman wind, waste landscapes.
My watcher glares contempt
as I slog through ruts, voices,
to wake: to pacify. The Task.

Colour Key

For under the big yellow one:
percent of skin coverage.
For into the blue:
business comfort with free drinks.
Whites on Sunday
for a thousand bowling-greens
while wasters in parlours
try not to pocket the black
and the Grim One rides trams.

For ones in the red
there are rates of repayment
but for superpowers in a clinch
the wrestle for our blue planet
will suddenly break into waltzes
for the little red one!

Are they quoting odds?
No, no promises
for into the big, big dark.

A 1988 news item flagged international co-operation for research into the planet
Mercury.

Bin

Keys, rags, plastic flowers, tickets, ash
follow each other into the bin. Also gadgetry
that gives no satisfaction. But there is no bin
we are not in. Over the unvalued earth
outside Tomsk, trailing a rating of 7,
floats a reminder that becomes the future
blight. A cloud, a little cloudy sky-bin
cradling its message, which it is bursting to blab.

Terror

THE EMISSARY, 2002

Terror is the alert face of the well-informed USIS intern
freshly flown in from the States. Over canapés I learn
she's hot on a project, workshops on "the world-wide concern

we all feel". When I query what woes we share, her primed pose
confirms the post-September-eleventh atmosphere round the
    gateaux:
this posting she's focused on Terror, Terror her mission to disclose.

WITH CARE

The boy dead by the wall, the girl mangled—
not fingered by disease nor wasted by mischance;
just nameless kids piled in a restaurant,
with the perpetrator. The media call his score,
then look for coverage and switch identity on
to find them names. And he—he stalked his moment
and company, in detestation and fear,
alone—trained on his target with killing care.

Care planned his one-way trip, care built his bomb,
armoured and geared his mind. And other care
cast him among the rejected, gave him eyes
to see power perched in tank-turrets, power abroad
on diplomatic stairs, in bank-towers, draining the world
of ordinary pride and work, and trampling lives.

KNIFE IN HEAD

In the heads of millions it is found—
knife in head.
The barb of injustice nests there.
It turns and festers.

This man has queued
for days at the check-point.
His family needs food and medicine.
On the other side is work.
More buildings for a rich nation.
On his side, foreigners
snatch land and build.
Foreign troops in tanks
plough up streets, homes,
livelihood, memories.
In the wrecked market
anger enters at the eyes
invades the brain
seats the blade
drives the point home:
nothing can staunch his shame
but the dead he'll claim, the body-count.
Knife in head.

This girl is a student.
In her angry city
her brothers are out throwing stones
at the tanks of the occupying forces—
for them, no chance
of safety, good years, travel.
Her people have stopped listening
for those rumours of a sound-track

from a receding planet.
Her cousin one year older
became a dead hero.
People in her street have been killed.
She straps the explosive packets under her breasts.
For her, no wedding, but a name
in the lengthening list of martyrs.
Every day will heap dust on her sacrifice.
The bus pulls up
full of the justified—
people with high fences,
people who can travel everywhere.
She moves up the aisle and sits
next to a woman with a child.
Knife in head.

GRIEF FOR THE VICTIMS OF THE BALI BOMBING, OCTOBER 2002

The leaving was not grief.
Holiday rang in their laughter
at the airport gate.
They were ours in their holiday gear:
your schoolfriend, his sister,
the neighbour's son.
And all to return with a tan
and memories and the best photos ever.
Now they stand
beyond the gate in a year
they will not re-enter,
or pause by the shattered sill.
They are the bitterly mourned.
They have become
the family of everyone.

They have left their photos uninhabited.
They have left the allotment of years untaken.
Their laughter was snatched away, their plans shrivelled
to history in the monstrous updraught of hate.
We who wait, alone must keep their appointments.

NEWS EVERY HALF HOUR
When every news flash tells us many die
unjustly, or that millions can't be fed,
who's letting blood today, who's being bled
is hard to tell. Here's this atrocity—
who did it, who knew what, and what they said
is all we have to judge the matter by.
Who paid which piper, in what currency,
how in whose history-books it will be read
in the age-long war of words, and just how cred-
ible any of that is—what they're trying to hide,
what means what end is supposed to justify—
the treadmill turns beneath the staggering tread.
That's life. The world goes horrified to bed
and in the morning rises horrified.

Abu Ghraib

Every atrocity
is a musical waiting to be made.
A musical, because
it makes money.
A musical, because
behind the numbers
fans may omit to hear
grunts, shrieks,
the burning backdrop,
streets of the dying city.
The pause before the strike.
A musical, because the poses
need no translation,
no-one asks why
the guy from the stage-door
is impaling the mezzo,
no-one apologises
for a musical
and the final word is always
Say cheese.

Some Politicians

To have preached even for a moment
that money matters
more than the good it buys,
to have proclaimed the end of caring,
to have unmothered the State
and left orphans to the wind,

to have waged phony battle
on the homeless and fugitive,
the needy come to our door,
to have danced on a tally of the drowned,
to have pursued the desperate
for electoral triumph —

these are your names
on the sea-bed at our shore gate
behind razor wire
among the fatherless
the trapped and the destitute
and among the separated families.

The Asylum-Seekers

Bearing your loss
however you can
to our fearful ports
       NO PLACE
       my abasement
Your cry in my hearing
your children your children
the salt waste
these depths these deaths
       my abasement
Your feet in my shallows
your hands at my shore
my guns at your face
inquisition
       NO PLACE
your plea in my ear
your need in my sight
rights and denial
undoing of lives
       NO PLACE
my guards in your path
your grief in my soul
the pledges broken
time passing time passing
       my abasement

Boat Voices

PALAPA: KAI NOLTE
lifted the first survivor—a child—to safety at 2.30pm. The rescue
continued all afternoon to the rhythm of the swell. Nolte said after a
while "This is just like fishing".

Kai Nolte lifted the first survivor—a child—
to safety at 2.30pm. So see him
one step up from the abyss, this
first stay in the human chain, angel
of the bringing-forth, its physicality,
exulting! He it is alights on the promise
the deep makes, the shoal shining, eyes
beyond the margin's predictable lives.
His arm at stretch now, assurance of resurgence,
his the sea-errand. *The rescue continued*
all afternoon to the rhythm of the swell.

Fishers of men, here found so, endowed
with strength in the prime, captained to rebuff
powers, and stood hours-long handing them
up—the child to his second life—hands
in sight everywhere, hands from the sea,
seized—the woman made rags by despair,
rising—and eyes met, the answering.
Nolte said after a while "This is just like fishing".
Not all of life to most men carries such
nor surely to you, Norwegian mariner
lowest on the ladder, such a draft again.

Kai Nolte was a sailor on the Norwegian ship, the *Tampa*, which picked up asylum-
seekers from the sinking Palapa in the India Ocean. Italicised sentences are from
newspaper reports.

TAMPA: CAPTAIN ARNE RINAAN

*looked down on the deck. "You could see it from the bridge, they
started to be restless, started looking at the stars, the wind direction
changed, everything changed."*

On deck in the dark
between containers
families are asleep.
They have passage.
Outcast panic is past
and shipwreck past.
God's compass is set
for the ancient land of Beach,
Australia.

High on the bridge
their world's heartbeat
god can glance down
storeys to the pit.
His hand to save
his will to landfall
holds firm, they sleep.

Till a shadow crosses the screens,
a contrary will clamps
its hand on his—
and these know
who learned to steer
by stars, smelt winds,
do not forget powers
that change course,
that coerce and condemn.

Lost or saved
turning in their slerep
in the belly of the whale
the ship's turning
wakes them, they know
it all, their universe
turns in the waters
and the continents turn
to inurn them—

their lit beach
of the captain's will to save
flares and recedes
bleeds a trace
into voids of hate
is gone—

they rouse, they leap up—

round them powers move—tides
of legislation rise
on the expensively shod and exercised
feet of politicians
in the skateboard arena
minds of politicians
making their mark
keeping their footing
saving their skins
figuring the gradient
of the electoral chicane
turning their trick
and professionally
mouthing family

chanting security
painting a picture
about difference

and however the people
rail and insist on a course
and however the captain in his honour
prevails in his course
they are lost on these seas
and this sand

and for long, long
under the lash of chance
they will find no landfall
beached in a container
for as many years as it takes
the scorn of commandants
in Australia.

WILLIAM STREET: ERIC VARDARLIS
*wept. "[This is] open game [season] on refugees. If they come near
our shores, the government is going to push them out, tow them out,
drag them out. I can't believe this is happening in this country."*

It is open season on refugees
and some are fairer game than others.
Their lawyer is weeping in William Street.

You can hardly expect an MP to greet
a muslim, a spic and a black as brothers.
Illegal's the word for refugees.

The PM tells us, expect a fleet

of indigent terrorists under cover.
They'll blow up your neighbourhood street by street.

Fugitives jailed by our northern seas—
election-tactics for those who govern,
Canberra-deaf to refugees.

What of the forerunners they might meet?
"No more must come"—that's a Bosnian mother,
twelve years safe on her Melbourne street.

Baiting *illegals* is strategy.
Africans, Asians and such—why bother?
It is open season on refugees
and the bleeding hearts on William Street.

IN BRISBANE, JOHN HOWARD
called a press conference: "it was all carried out in accordance
with very careful legal advice … There was no violence. We gave
humanitarian assistance; we gave medical assistance; we particularly
looked after the person who'd had the child."
"Packages and services"—Scott Morrison, Minister for Immigration.

Very careful legal advice—
the armour of major criminals—
now shelters governments.

You can bomb a village to rubble
with your *very careful legal advice*
you can pauperise hundreds.

Citing *very careful legal advice*
you can lock a man away for decades

make children into mental cases
drive a sane man to set himself alight.

You can be a senior retired statesman
you can retain your honours
sport gewgaws from foreign states
you can die unimpeached.
Because who will speak for the least of these?

#

No violence is a phrase
to be measured against cattle prods
and photographs of burnt hands.

These political days
publicspeak is a code
not everyone may wish to understand.

#

Humanitarian assistance—passage to hell, food till landing?
Medical assistance—one blood pressure check and a few sanitary
    pads?
Packages, services, facilities, operatives endless and affectless
as the progeny of Eichmann, serviceable, faceless,
just look for a church-goer vowed to efficiency.
Implementation? No problem
for this automaton, basing
unthinkable cruelty
strictly on departmental information.

#

The person who'd had the child
has a name.
The child has a name.
The child has a mother (who is probably *the person*)
and maybe a father. Persons have fathers.
The child could be a son or perhaps a daughter.

Hope you looked after the child as well as *the person*.
The little daughter, let's guess, as well as the woman.
And perhaps the father too?

Martians landing mid-ocean
Martians who work by parthenogenesis
both sexes (or indeterminates) bearing young (probably also
    indeterminate)
processed out of their think-glands or space-bling
might thus describe the event
happening to a woman with lustrous eyes, pretty slippers, sweaty
    wraps, aching back, bleeding womb,
small souvenirs of her village tucked away in her home-woven bag,
    carefully wrapped photographs of her murdered brothers and
    her mother she couldn't bring with her (will she ever see her
    again?),
a woman who hopes against hope to see her little one (the daughter
    or son) run among trees in the wind calling for joy, a woman
    who fears drowning—
sexless Martians documenting the expedition might see her as
The person who'd had the child
to be *particularly looked after*—
Locked up? Separated from her husband? Placed where no-one
    speaks her language?

No answers.
We are not to know
what is done in our name.

Because who can prevail for the least of these?

SIEV X: A SURVIVOR

Everywhere children were drowning ... Those still alive saw bodies
all around them, they littered the water. Wherever you looked, said
one survivor, "you see dead children like birds floating on the water".

Like birds floating on the water
the drowned children wash up
on the mind's beach. *Everywhere*
children were drowning

and the politicians finding
a prayer for the new morality:
save us from the dead children
and their silent landfall.

The sea gives up its innocents.
Buried or not buried,
uncomforted, unnamed,
they drift on inland.

Secure in our sunlight, we
survivors endure the *dead*
children like birds floating
as spaces among us.

These the new Australians
will never draw up to our table,

will never walk tall in our cities.
They have no memorial

but the love that could not hold them
and the care that was their due.
Each night floods our shores
with their sodden wings.

S.S. TOBRUK: A SENIOR NAVAL OFFICER
"There's two hatches open ... I thought 'It's like a slave ship,' I
thought 'Jesus, I thought we were Australians. I thought we were a
good bloody country.' "

I'm walking the deck in whites. A career
with traditions and service and discipline,
and sea to the very horizons' rim.
There's my idea, it's simple and clean,

except there are depths. You live this life
and another one opens underneath,
like today, down the cavernous hatch, I've seen
what I used to think was a working hive

but the upturned rows on rows of faces
restless and hopeless, with prison to come—
there it was, a plate I scanned once, from
a history of transatlantic slavers.

Slave-ships were carefully diagrammed.
The maximum pay-load under hatches
called for measuring, averages
of height and width. Sickness, mortality,

low diet. Births? If they died on the way
there'd be places vacant. They overstocked,
it'd all work out by the time they docked.
Losses, profits—yes, it was trade.

But we provide stretchers—we're humane.
Opening hatches in tropical weather
is good form too. We're in this together
except I'm on deck, mulling the pain

of an age-old puzzle: why me, why them?
They're political scandal, they're cattle
that broke their fences and tried to scatter
fleeing from want and harm, to a dream

of belonging. My own grandfather came
on a boat, with one change of clothes, a Bible.
How was he different from this rabble?
He was white, and British. He hailed from Home

and not in distress; a sort of adventure,
empire building, perhaps with luck
a good life founded on honest work—
their hope, these families headed for hell

in our hold, on Australia's order. I took
a fair go from Dad, and Mum said heart.
For a new free country, not a bad start.
And that's how I thought we were. Now look.

THERE ARE NO WORDS FOR THIS

Let the young man hang.
Let children lose their trust.
Let them despair and run amuk.
And send them back.

Let the woman lose hold of her child
on the deep, among known bodies.
Let oceans take as flotsam
these lives.

1835: a captain—saved—
leaves his shipful of women
to drown off Boulogne, not one
alive, taken off—

his orders being to land them
in New South Wales. What's changed?
Let oceans take them, or slavers.
Or years damn them.

It's simple: they're different. Plus,
illegals, they chose their fates:
there are words for it—human waste.
And the words for us?

A Picture of Ilham Tohti

A picture of this Uyghur writer sentenced in a Chinese court to life imprisonment for "separatism", was placed in the Empty Chair at the 2014 PEN Congress.

The writer in the empty chair looks at me.
He looks at me out of his troubled eyes.
He looks at me out of the day of his arrest.
He looks at me out of a past hour,
the hour of the rest of his life.
He looks at me out of the jeers, the rifle-butts, the prison
(he did not know that when this image was made).

He looks at me out of his broken life.
He looks at me out of his persecuted family.
He looks at me out of his banned language.
He looks at me out of his destroyed books,
out of the one never to be published.
He looks at me out of his betrayed nation.
He looks at me out of his humanity.

He looks at me. The word after his last written word
struggles to breathe between us.
He looks at me, silenced. The world's voices die.
He is an image on cardboard placed on the chair
where the man would have leaned
crossing his legs, riffling his MS, smiling a little,
live, a man of words ready to read.

The Murdered Child

For the child boxed in up the stairs—
the world a whim turned off
by hands of resentment,
her Dad rattling on
in his life of sex and beer,
his glance a weight, a shove
aside, and the woman's slaps
and pummeling, her sneers—
    was there beauty?

Was there a leaf springing?
A schoolbook cover, shiny?
A path after rain? Did a wind
pick up litter like play?
And the grin on the kid that passed
her wheelchair, odd days,
did it send her heart skittering
like possibility? like a friend?
    Was there beauty?

No, the sour looks closed in.
The world went outside.
Noone came for hours.
Trying to think dancing.
Kindness: a memory of nurses.
The looks wrong when they came.
The stone at her heart, huge.
Bone fragments in scrubland.
    And beautiful tributes.

Chavez

To die in office, to die in Venezuela:
this was a last achievement. Chavez dead
shows the gringo phrase-mongers how to "stay the
course"—news flings his naming, never unsaid,
of the devilry of the self-proclaimed world's armed cop,
the endless interventions in the name
of Congress's over-hyped "well-defended democ
racy"—Mexico, Grenada—a muscled-up bully's game.

Not to die—that was his last wish, not dignified,
but surely granted by history's dictat
and in the hearts of the humble. Let journos deride,
this was a jaguar in his habitat,
this was a patriot's wiliness and pride—
to manifest people's power inviolate.

On the Telephone Tree

Richmond State Secondary College siege, November 1993

I am a leaf on a school siege
telephone tree.
The sap zings,
the phone starts ringing.
The chainsaw's sizing us up,
come in glossy.

Seven-thirty, I park.
They're occupying their school.
The school gates are chained.
I haul me over, and someone's
on the door and locks it behind me.
"In there."

Eight people. Then twelve.
By 8am we're edging thirty.
We've stopped getting coffee.
Do the cops mean it this time?
This is how you get arrested,
now decide who.

They've been here a year,
nearly. You can pick overnighters,
they can't raise a flicker.
Sunless, dumped
in reach of the telephone tree
by glum conscience,

them and the kids, learning
who's still on-site and with it
eleven months into the shredding
of forests of schools. Someone's
got to say what stays, what grows
and whose

are the roots driven deep.
You can feel the timber harden.
Police are tactics.
At the end of the day
someone's going to have the say.
Decide who.

Back in Brisbane, April 1985

In memory of John Manifold, 1915–1985

IN MY CITY

I am here under disabilities
in my city that murmurs to me on a cool night
through its hail-shattered louvres of a kid's sleepout.

I am here with my childhood
where backyards promise unending life
of flowering rain-fed vines, of family, of memory,

in my city
where stone upon stone makes no abiding city,
for history here is censored and torn down at midnight.

HISTORY: A CHECK-LIST

In case you forget
history drops in, goes to bed with you.
The night wind on the back steps remembers
the convicts gone bush.
The cop stopping a boy on his walk home after the last bus
to be searched up against a fence
remembers the Moreton Bay settlement.
The acts of harrassment.
The murdered commandant
bandied between the blacks and the convicts.
Things done behind galvanized iron fences.
The profit motive. Authority.
The windowless cells.
The tropical knights.
The cedar gone to matchwood over the falls.

The boys getting out of order.
The girl's body raped and dumped
bandied between the police and No Suggestions.
New estates on floodland.
The protection racket that needs protecting.
The Border toast.
The teenage pregnancies.
Honours sought in office.
People meeting in parks prepared for a night in the cells.
The sale proceeding in secret.
The signature obscured.
The Square prostituted.
The river-bank masked.
The teachers guyed in pronouncements of politicians.
Files stolen for future use.
The nights of rain and mould.
The Aborigines bandied between jurisdictions.
The road stabbed through rain-forest
bleeding the slow-built soils.
The river rising for its harvest
to find the speculators gone,
its revenge fences, the family furniture
and the woman on a bean-bag with her dog
trying to cross a flooded creek.

A TOUR OF TRIVIA
History is also a desert plaza—
eye of the city, a bricked well's
bronze version of the Queen

rather small, in possession of a clutch-bag.
She interprets the baked void square,
viewing askance her Parliament

whose hucksters in limousines treat the Police,
set the Press obedience trials
and dine with kickbacks;

set spies, stack polls, squint at education,
clear sites for enterprise
and new urbanity—

landscapes of old shade and shelter
spread unconsidered, ravished of fig and mangrove
for the embrace of concrete,

where passengers once walked to save the horse
'trained athletes' haul
the lolling travellers,

and the visiting tenor
(paid to be Jonah, his whale-jaw the stepped seating)
sings muck in King George Square.

It pays.

For the gifts of educators
are valued for their contribution to earnings from tourism,

and girls in frilled orchid two-pieces
are using their talents to water-ski in formation
by waterfront units for the camera.

JOHN MANIFOLD REMEMBERED
But my mother the university
stands to welcome her children
in the wide-cast bend of the unpolitical river

and honours herself as she honours her adopted son
who knew living must be political,
music and poetry is a slow deep politics.

John Manifold, who was our other university,
living his ideals,
hawking *The Tribune* on Saturdays,

roaring ballads for the workers
on a midden of chips from a bush balalaika,
tuning a love-sonnet to nylon fishing-line;

a long bus-route from Centre
soldier and Communist Manifold
estranged from grazier forebears—the people his reason—

sets Realist Writers on,
scores songs for Ballad Nights, sits poets, kids, neighbours
to mandolines, bush bass and lagerphone.

Manifold at the nursing-home, struck down,
shuffling, the mover still,
urges wood-carving tools on 'lazy old men'.

The centre is towards Manifolds', the wind off the Bay,
the bared-river-flats and the Wynnum weatherboard
and the hawk seen flying.

TWO DOCTORATES
Two belches of a politician in office
shrivelled the academics' resolve.
They are balancing this year's budget.

The lilt of a ballad pulls like memory,
a rifle-band shouldered, a hat in the ring,
tides of history, gleams on the Bay.

Honoured they were, robed, cited in one day
like stanza trailing stanza—John's
gone, I'd say, to shun the company.

It is no further in the giving of doctorates
from politics to politicking
from honour to dishonour

in my city.

Premier Bjelke-Petersen and John Manifold were awarded doctorates by the
University of Queensland. "A Hat in the Ring" is the title of an early satire (and
manifesto) in heroic couplets by John Manifold, published in *Selected Verse* (1948).

The Millennium

The night of the millennium.
Swift as thought,
jets from the city fireworks—
one slips, one rises.
2000! give or take a year,
since the star of peace,
since our hero lifted his arms
of a newborn, softer than down,
smoother than water.

Above Hamilton Beach
in flying-fox dark
it might as well be the age
ago of my childhood,
it might as well be the yesterday
before sails on the coast—
but for the frogs gone,
but for the huge immigrant
water-rats.

On the verandah friends
from their postwar schoolyears
are silent watchers
of their lives' passing—
assembled from interestate flights
and back with the smell of mangoes,
remnant mangroves of the river mouth
and the coursing, always, among ridges
of the river.

Beyond its dark expanse

in the insect-filled electric night
the city wakes to neon
ads, venues, traffic
and the breeze
along sombre parked-up streets.
Fifty years
between us and our inner lives,
the children we were.

All the moves
out, away from beginnings
into our public selves
still point back, back
to the wartime backyard,
the flooded air-raid shelter,
the hard-dug victory garden,
the now-unthinkable
incinerator,

the swing Dad made,
the climb over the cubby
bougainvillea
crossing above the gateway
to the forbidden house-roof
way above traffic,
the flowering frangipani's
grey-branched perches
for a child away in her reading.

Long mornings, longer
afternoons paused on childhood,
the subtropical coast waiting
for the next cyclone.
The sky-wide

fig-tree shade remembering
tides of heat, skies convulsed, deluge,
the river rising
leviathan—

days and generations
there, somehow, together
as never in the ordered tracts
of making a living. And always
the voice-beneath deep-running river-reach
of shipmen and river-dwellers,
the millennial light-foot tribesmen,
walkers,
and us watching;

here at its junction
with flash-flood occasion
(the now-slowing flares)
as we turn in the eddy, tides
of a sacred third river,
night-wind memory,
yield up their wreckage:
the corner shops, the dirt verges
gone under concrete,

the long way to school—
the neighbour with milk-bottles,
the gravel, the long grass,
the bus-stop, the new house, the loony,
the shack swamped
in outrageous morning glory,
the lit faces, the buried families,
heading with us under new numbers
into the kindly dark.

Weather, Times, Places

Weather from the College Windows

WINTER SKY, MELBOURNE
Melbourne has mountains!
Piled-up grey walls off endearing blue
and morning's red eye strikes west.

The tower on Sunday:
sleepers shun windows north that fling first
bird-skerries to the airport.

The cloud-range crumbles.
Wind tears inshore and whaleback hummocks
surface under a blown sky,

day-faring buildings
braced east pull on their pale shirts. Melbourne
relinquishes cloud ramparts

whose retinue (blue
as the Bight) move off behind Parkroyal,
link up with the Buller skiers.

EPICS ENACTED IN CLOUD
Low squadrons' blackened darts
faster than the tiny plane cross mighty western draughts.

Transparent policy
throws them desperately south: tatters and smudges flee.

Ruddiness in glow and gout
of a fire burned low, the lights of a civilisation go out.

The sky of threat
rushes to a knot—

its craze of cavernous battery and burnished torture
delight of historians!

There culture-heroes circle
breathing hard, citing the reasons, destiny's work,

till the swirl begins to clear
and washed levels measure a new era.

(It is all mindless, mindless!)
The near birds' piping

will pass for peasant song and dance;
they take their harvest.

Straight as the flight-log's line
a messenger from outland drops

exactly on the darkening map
and new-raised columns drag the plain.

Hiroshima? Chernobyl? This is a view from the tower, out.
Not seasons' chemistry set cloud to murder the planet.

LONGITUDES
On the city horizon
the cables of the great cranes are set swinging

by wind out of the north.
And the ruffs and hillocks and wave-tops of whole

avenues go up and over, unsettled days now.
Smaller phenomena

take an airing:
retina-scorch of a tilted window's rectangle turns out

not to be Mayday in September,
just a gap in clouds' coursing and curdling;

the plane-tree's stripling yellow twigs
zig-zag and jostle and tower

and thrash above the boughs' wallow;
paired on drying tennis-courts, like navigators

plotting on the run, in mid-ocean dark
each day's wind-force——weeks of it——

players see serves pitch short, throws spray from vertical,
a wild spring day.

Four Tales

A HEADACHE COMING ON

She walked up the stairs counting. She had never till then noticed
how solid, how very solid they were. It would take a workman to
open up the space under them—none of the wood had shifted in
seventy years. She worried again, walked down and round the side
and stood still, just looking: panelling, banisters, rail, lifetimes
of rubbing the wax in, polishing. Why had her mother had this
secrecy, this need to hide something—

She decided on a cup of coffee. She could feel a headache, a bad
one, coming on.

UNWRAPPING THE COLOURS

He unwrapped the box, which turned out to be dark green with a
picture of cows, black and white ones, on the front. It did not seem
much of an advertisement for crayons: black, white and green with
a sky of mild blue, that was all. Shoving the paper into the bin, and
the coloured string, he sat down. How many colours? The end of the
box read

REGGLES FINE COLOURS

thirty-six crayons for artists

Made in Australia

He was pleased he'd chosen Australian. The lid fitted quite tightly.
He prised it up and laid it on the table. The crayons were not round
but square and were, he found, good to hold. Each one was wrapped
in paper with a seal, rather like a cigar seal, drawn on it. One end
of the paper above the seal said REGGLES and the other end gave
the name of the colour. He read the names with interest. Sienna,
he read, Vermilion, Crimson, Ochre, Olive, Viridian, Ultramarine.
These seemed to him very beautiful names. After all, the entire
visible world could be created from them. Then he saw that one

crayon had no name: REGGLES, seal, blank, that's what was
printed on it. He felt confused. Should he ask for his money back?

Turning the crayon to look at its point he thought it rather
uninteresting: a pale colour, greyish perhaps, maybe mauve, though
the longer he looked the more he detected a sort of greenish tinge.
He put it down very carefully. The colours as he reviewed them
sounded like a sky before hail. Then he remembered what it was
really like, this crayon: it reminded him of the family where the
middle child had no name.

SHE AND HE WOULD RATHER BE

You will not, he said, tell my child fairy stories.

She laughed back. My mother told us fairy stories every night of
our lives!

They're filthy decadent and frightening, he went on, they go on
about all the things a child should be protected from.

Oh that's ridiculous. What do you mean.

I mean death and fear, and death fear and sex all mixed up, he
answered smugly.

Don't be silly, she said, conscious that you couldn't argue against
a frightened child, especially if he wore a beard, not to speak of
a bow-tie. Do you mean a child needs to be protected from frog-
princes?

They're part of it, he said, meaning to leave her in suspense.

Well! I wish I'd met one, she retorted, trying not to laugh. At
least frogs know fairy tales are good for you! They might change
you into something else, something you'd rather be.

THE RIVER RISING

The little party of explorers had been calm too long. Now, too
suddenly, they became desperate. They had long noticed the heat
increasing, the animals, even savage ones, gathering and then

scattering, and around them the many unmapped channels of the river rising. The swamps that stretched to the horizon had become a sea. There was no overnight transformation. So quiet, gradual and benign were these unaccustomed landscapes, green and spacious, that they were in the end taken by surprise, yet their eyes had been open—strained open, you could say, to observe—the whole time.

An Excursion: Some Colombian Poems

THE MOVELESS SEA OF THE LLANOS
Translated from the Spanish of Oscar Echeverri Mejía

You don't have to tell me it's the sea. That I knew
from the herons dreaming of their sails. From the palm-grove
    islands
lifting their tall masts.
I sensed it
from the horizon holding the sky up on arms of mist,
from the sun sinking
to die in the arms of the anguished sea of grass
and the sun rising
reborn, like a great sea-beacon.

You don't have to tell me it's the sea. I felt it
in the hot waves of pasture that invade the beaches
like a crazed great vegetable tongue. In the wind's murmur
tasting of salt. In the little streams
that creep through the plain and pour out their waters.
In the sea-gulf of the Meta.
In the strange siren-songs—
ship's sirens and sirens of flesh and bone—
you hear there in the night. In the shipwreck
of things living and not living, every sunset.

I know it now: it is sea,
I asked for no proofs
seeing how the Meta drowns in its huge waves
how the plainsman steers among its endless currents
and stays afloat,

how the young bull—miraculous amphibian—
nibbles stars in its crystalline glass,
how the horse runs on through its ecstatic waves of green
with his mane like a ship's rigging.

Yes, it is sea, a sea not named on maps, alive with creatures
made in its image and likeness.
The sea where men and animals sink
and where the sun and moon are born, each in its own way.

I know beyond all doubt, it is sea
and I too am inside its spell
like the rider, like the young bull, like heron and parrot,
like palm and snake and monkey,
like the water coursing its grassy entrails.

This is the sea and now I can never forget
its lessons of sun and solitude,
its daily toil, destroying and creating,
its mighty surges of heat, of death and life,
its green storms,
its calm times and its vegetable dreaming,
the calls—symphonies even—of its animals.

Sea of the great Plain, I am coming back to you,
because my fate as a sailor of the earth
tells me that here I shall keep some day my tryst with water.

From *Grief and Hardship*, Cali 1974

THE MAN MURDERED IN THE DARK

Translated from the Spanish of Oscar Echeverri Mejía

I am the one they murdered in the dark.
Death spread the whole
length and breadth of my body.
I am darker than night. But
less so with time, and in the earth
who knows what space I fill,
more unknown than death itself.

I am the one they murdered in the dark.
Nobody knows my name; even I have forgotten it.
There won't be flowers put on my tomb
because I haven't earth enough
even to cover my bones.
Nobody mourns my dying
since nobody cares that I was alive.

I am the one they murdered in the dark.
No bells toll for my death
because it's off the record. I was no-one, I am no-one
and I have no tombstone
and no name written on it—
if I had one, it's been rubbed out.

I am the one they murdered in the dark.
My death has been nameless, same as my life.
No-one is calling me; anyway I hear nothing. No-one
is searching for me in the folds of the earth
because no-one cares. (Only God knows me.)

And as my ashes go back to the land
And I turn into sap,
I'm forgetting that I ever had a life
Because for the world I was only
The one they murdered in the dark!

From *Grief and Hardship*, Cali 1974

ALONG THE CAUCA RIVER

Translated from the Spanish of Jaime Jaramillo Escobar

We used to go down—me and my horse—twice a year to the Cauca
River.
Down out of the high mountains we'd go and at daybreak we'd
catch sight of the river
among black rocks and clumps of palms, and it was great to see the
river.
We'd be travelling at night in August, by moonlight, or else in
winter, one January or another,
But my horse knew the track by heart or just made it up anyway.
He was the one who traced it—I couldn't see a thing.
I was thirteen, my horse was five years old, we were very young to
be taking that road by ourselves.
What a mate my horse was, cleverer and better trained than I was,
And yet it was I who held the reins,
Simply because I was the son of the horse's owner, that's the way
things are.
I'd give him lumps of sugar in my hand, facing him, gazing at him,
And I never played him the dirty trick of emptying beer over his
head, crowned with the two twitching ears.
I'd call him by his full name and he'd come at a sweet, gentle trot,
And pick his way down into the gully of the riverbed where the
mist hadn't yet lifted, but lay in the thickets of reeds, grey and
shining with dew at six in the morning.

As we went along, I'd do all the poems of Porfirio Barba-Jacob for
my horse, the ones that mooched around wild mountain country.
I don't remember my horse having anything to say about the poems,
but if I stopped declaiming, he'd stop.
Of course, before we started I'd have washed him down,
I'd have walked him out in the yard behind the house, feeding him
sugar-cane, honey and bran, peeled bananas,
Combed him, and stroked him, and slapped his rump,
Groomed him thoroughly and combed his mane and tail with care
And looked to the gear: the red saddle-rug for his back, the polished
bridle, the smooth firm girth, the saddle all decorated with carving
and silver, the stirrups of worked copper, the leather jacket, my felt
hat. Right up till the moment I jammed the hat on my head, the
horse simply wouldn't let us start.
My father would be keeping an eye on everything, very quietly and
seriously,
And if every detail was right he approved with a nod.

I know that this horse died way back and for me to be still living is
unfair.
He was a white horse with a long mane, called Don Palomo
Jaramillo.
The Cauca River knows nothing of all that because it comes from
far, far away, from the great plains of grass,
So calm, full of really big fish—back then—
The river that had flowed between banks where the blacks drank in
their palm shelters,
Where they lived in huts, worked, or didn't work, fought one
another with huge forks of galvanised steel, Cornet brand,
Blacks who'd poured their blood into the river, their sweat, their
tears,
Who feted Sunday in the ports, each port with its railway-station
and those green Pilsener bottles for their thirst, their need to drink,
for their fighting spirit.

At Anza, you had to cross the wild river in a canoe, holding up the
horse's head with the bridle so he wouldn't drown.
The horse would labour along, but still, he'd keep going against the
rush of the water.
My horse watched me throwing back rotgut, and said nothing.
He took me home drunk, he caressed me with his muzzle, with the
side of his head.
He'd stand steady, look at me, and say: Come on.
He galloped with mane straining the wind to delight me,
Or carried me carefully over bad tracks, those winters.
Now I have no horse and have to go by car, I live inside it
completely out of touch.
Landscape moving at a hundred ks an hour has neither head nor
tail and no-one can tell why it makes them feel sick,
But my horse knew about landscapes, he was a horse for landscapes,
A horse just born of a horse, but grander than the Queen's Rolls
Royce.

The best river in the world is the first river, the one where we went
in naked,
And the rest are just other rivers, like other women and other
friends.
If the Magdalena River didn't speak to me when I was a boy, why
should it speak now; might as well not try.
I talked long with the Cauca River and it told me everything,
The same things the Magdalena could have told me,
But the Cauca put a hand on my shoulder and spoke in my ear
And I didn't like the other so much because its talk was shouting.
I went down with friends to the Cauca and we swam across, at Anza,
at Cangrejo, Tulio Ospina, La Pintada, Cali,
But I never swam across the Magdalena anywhere.
The Magdalena tried to drown me, raise up waves and pull me
under; when I waved an arm it shoved me down. Yes, I'm scared of
the Magdalena.

On the banks of the Cauca I'd go back and forth like a king among his people.
At the Bolombolo Bridge I could just talk with passers-by, with a friend, with the lonely night.
The Bolombolo Bridge disappeared under the waters of a dam,
And with it the houses and the big iron-roofed pubs.
The name Bolombolo will last for ever in the poems of Leon de Grieff,
Who actually saw the port begin, when they built the railway.
The smell of coal is gone, it disappeared with the trains, all that's left is whores
Who'll soon disappear under the dam waters, and billiard tables with their feet in the air, the restaurants that served hot soup, and my police-inspector's revolver.
Over the Bolombolo Bridge one night I chased a bandit, the bandit jumped in the river, I shot a round in the air so I could get talking about it over beers with the lieutenant.

Water of the Cauca,
Water I'm drinking right now from fine crystal glasses: yellowish, discoloured, pretty dirty really—
If my horse were here to drink you, he'd drop down dead.

Jaime Jaramillo Escobar *Selecta*, Tercer Mundo Editores, Bogotá, 1987, pp. 17–21.

PORFIRIO BARBA-JACOB

Translated from the Spanish of Jaime Jaramillo Escobar
For José Alvarez Patiño

Porfirio Barba-Jacob sending out shouts all over America,
Primitive desperate shrieks, birthing-screams,
That would horrify the educated Mr Eliot, that true gentleman.
Porfirio hatless, like the Furies, showing no respect for the
neighbourhood,
Porfirio in eruption, flinging out burning rocks and dirt all over
America,
Bald, shaggy, waving his arms like a windmill;
Surely they won't have let him into heaven, going on like that.
And yet he was a loner, too, among the flames and sulphur,
A site of upheaval, carried away, hounded by it, a demon of energy,
Running me down with a great terrible howling,
Leaving here for other parts as if he were the gale
That at one moment subsides and turns gentle among frail beings
And then at another, tumultuous and confused as head-waters
bursting from the earth.
Passionate, never still, storming about,
So that all that noise, all the roaring shook my nerves.
But he believed he had to roar, a backblocks American,
Bellowing like one possessed, capering, shouting the whole time,
Dragging round a pain that was simply too great,
Punching up everyone,
Cranky, ear-splitting, distraught, ashen-faced,
Now at a trot, now at a gallop,
Why all that rushing back and forth, to wear himself out with
cursing.
Better to shut up and sit still in front of the TV.
Just too many questions for the single throw-away answer,
And that full-throated rhetoric of his times, which complicates
things.

After shocking us all, inconsiderately—red alarm, the maximum—
And pounding our front door (this is a respectable house) with pile-
driver blows,
He all at once stood still, just gazing on the countryside,
The tree casting its shade, the lamb grazing, the wind in the
branches overhead.
And yet there was need of all that force to show us his reality and
our own.
Without his stentorian shout, in those peaceable between-wars
years, we mightn't have found out anything about anything.
Still, why does he shove us along at exactly the worst moment,
Just when we're getting to the point where the road peters out?

Jaime Jaramillo Escobar, *Selecta*, Tercer Mundo Editores, Bogotá, 1987.

WAYS TO WASTE TIME

translated from the Spanish of Jaime Jaramillo Escobar

The magnate who wastes time producing, tells the rest they waste it
using.
Time's not days in a row, just the same one again and again—the
ancients had no time for time.
The priest says give it up to God, the whole lot's his.
Authors say, use it to read their marvellous books.
Film-makers—get the picture—nothing else matters.
Musos figure time's too short to hear all the music.
Travel agents advertise—travel eats time in style—
and the State keeps regulating, it's the nation we owe our time to.
The beloved, she's put in a claim for every minute.
But me, just one of these days, I'd like time for myself.
As for my father, never wasting a moment—he'll pick up his
savings in eternity.

Jaime Jaramillo Escobar, *Selecta*, Tercer Mundo Editores, Bogotá, 1987, p. 95.

SONNET TO THE SONNET

Translated from the Spanish of Jaime Jaramillo Escobar

You—yes, it's you I'm on about—who of old
was perfection, the model, the high point, treasury
of the most glorious highly-rated poetry
basking in public honours and princely benison,

who in the hands of Shakespeare took up
from those of Petrarch the blushing garland of roses,
and in Quevedo and Villegas opened to the sun
whatever could not be brought to life by Lope,

you—always you—so full of your ideas,
you were the one chosen by worthy citizens
for your dissembling face and your sly habits

and when you lost your mystery and your secrets,
there you were stark naked, pawed-over and sad,
with no charms left but your two three-liners

and your cheeky tail!

Jaime Jaramillo Escobar Selecta, Tercer Mundo Editores, Bogotá, 1987. p.114.

RECYCLING

Translated from the Spanish of Piedad Bonnett

When my dad had a fit of madness and killed the cat
my cat Bartolo
because he stuck his tail in the soup
and because he was old and wasn't hunting rats like he should
and anyway he cost money to feed
when Dad got drunk and killed him with his own hands

there was pandemonium in the house
they all came all of them
my sister said keep the eyes for me
for a pair of ear-rings and Martino
our neighbour who was blind asked for the guts
to make strings for his violin
and my mum who wept first off wept with me
she wanted the fur
to put a collar on her jacket
and the whiskers
my brother Eladio who works on machines asked for them
and the pads of his paws were
beautiful pincushions
for the fat witch who lives behind the courtyard
sewing for people.
We boiled everything that was left with salt and onions
That went to Luis who sleeps up our lane
because even cat soup is good against hunger
Me I asked for the bones
I'm grinding them up one by one in front of my sister's mirror
because grannie says
anyone who touches bonedust turns invisible
And I'd like that

From *PEN International* Vol.54, No.2, 2004; 59.

The following three poems were written in poetry workshops. Working in pairs on prescribed topics (the titles), the poets alternately added a line without seeing what had been written before. They had to agree (again, without reading) when to finish. Only minimal adjustments were made later.

Travelling to the Dead Centre

We notice the abundance of living things.

Established cities hold cemeteries near their centre like prestigious suburbs.

Green things are smaller.

Even the stones crumble towards paths growing crowded, gregarious, winding about, making way for newcomers,

bus-loads envying the view of planes, plane-loads craving the 'atmosphere'.

Travelling through is a little like a visit to Disneyland, the Fairy Park at Anakie—

Oh, she said unhelpfully, it's dead, but it's not dead centre. If you see what I mean.

The dead can be remembered in bright eternal flowers, elaborate statuary. It is consoling that our tributaries to the dead can be so light, festive, fanciful—

the supplementary tank on radial roads—solid geometry of The Heart!

I used to walk from the university round the Melbourne cemetery, attractive as midnight to a child

—she knows there is still a centre to be visited—

I was amused by lines like Not dead, only sleeping.

Below—the soak, above—The Rock's hurrying ant-life.

Now I see that you need more compromise and compassion.

A neat expanse of green lawn?

Alternate lines by Judith Rodriguez and Meredith Jelbart

Tourists in the Pacific

The bus scrunches its rims through coral grit.
White people wander, wondering what it was like before, or if it was
or why it wasn't, and wait to go home . . .
(the natives could never be black enough for the reverend)
. . . and when they leave the parts their ancestors installed, suddenly it
is all uneasy and beautiful.
The consul boasts, Yvonne got a sycamore to grow—but they took to
it with machetes.
Each culture is totally different and each place seems like the last.
The bus is always too late to pick them up—it's the other reef they
wanted—
In the Pacific the gods have not yet left the earth—the visitors try to
touch them.
They fly the shells in, she says. The divers are spies—and did you
see—they never get sunburnt!
Pacific people are generous with their gods.
Not forgetting tourists—connections—lines out—bicycles even—
Spanish tourists looking for bulls in every cockfight—
sea-island cotton shredding and the Gaugins here bad copies of
something not now seen.
Australians see the ghosts of their neighbours.
The bookings are not correct, Mrs Wolfsohn, and you have not paid
for the walk from the plantation.
On the whole black Australians don't visit the Pacific.

Alternate lines by Judith Rodriguez and William Henderson

Tricycles for Geriatrics

Along the beach we move, the family on wheels

nuts, bolts, a vulcanising kit

My son in pram, my daughter on skates clinging to the handlebars, my father in his wheelchair

moving ahead—an interest in life

Sometimes my daughter rides my father's knee, plays with the gears and levers, takes him careering in tight circles to the fear of joggers, strolling families and sea-gulls

the latest spectacular road-deaths

He admires the children, expects them to be athletes

careering towards complicated premature grave-sites

Told to slow down at sixty-six, my father threw away his pills in pique, and pedalled his push-bike out along the river-bank, until he had a stroke

like the Scythian tribesmen, buried upright on their horses.

Alternate lines by Meredith Jelbart and Judith Rodriguez

La Perouse

Admirable, luckless La Perouse!
A suburb in an English colonial
secretary's city—the navigator
from remote Kamchatka could only
antedate and view the founding
and seal despatches for Paris.

Luck gave no credits for his frank
acknowledgment of Cook,
"first of navigators". The Pacific
whistled boats under in Lituva Bay,
broke out reefs under the walls
of ships. Then a second wreck.

He's history. The portrait rounds him
in braid, amiable, intelligent,
plump. For lack of iron
lashing palm to old boards
on a Samoan beach—Languedoc
gaunt as Yorkshire at the end.

Como

Now why are we here, gawking at décor
beyond our means, and wood and iron technology
so far behind our discreet machines we'd scorn it
even if we could use it and approved the solid
flower-press and candle-mould, scythe and mangle and goffer?
My Mum and your Nan can afford respect with their smiling
at irons on the hob and chamber-pots—they've survived them.

We are here to cluck at the non-restoration of gaslight,
and think of the dust in the ruched morning-room curtain—
is it original? The count-thread stitchery in samplers
and dolls' clothes made by little girls are, for certain;
our girls won't look at such fuss. The arts of furling
fans, and listing partners to dance, have receded
in the day of takeaway, fashion-labels, whiteware and Ikea,

and who now treats to have a dining-suite supplied
and settles on Richmond morticians who never touch
planks less than wrist-thick, whose whole ideal is "reliable"
and for polish, colour of tanned hide? Here we come
wondering how Armytages ever worried
among Ada's hunting-horn tableaux of sons and daughters,
billiard-room walls ribbed high with English oars,

receipts from country properties, lawns for croquet
and marquees at need. We're let off—the ease of museums!
It wasn't my uncle who died up-country of exposure
six years after grandfather's partner was speared,
it wasn't your Ethel who died at seven of diphtheria.
No-one was bankrupted so we could gape at the commode,
turn the girls' music and sigh for the built-over orchard.

Werribee

Ringbarked, the landscapes of success
rear a staircase second to none
on bluestone walls of importance,
so race-day conversation guests
can sink in a fancy ottoman.
The price of wool supports

hunting, a tower, imported busts,
marriage-settlements, sons' expenses,
ha-ha and lake, hunt balls,
though the bunya-pines they tried are stunted
and sons choose other residences;
the lake-water's gone, stocks fall

till the grand unmaintainable hulk's
a film-set, with everything catalogued.
But revving, rousing the gardens
great-grandsons top graziers' hustle
with route-maps, tweed caps, klaxons and goggles
at a rally of Aston-Martins!

Reasonable Procedure

The well-known bookseller Mr E.W.Cole advertised in The Herald for a wife. Despite his failure to keep a first appointment to meet, the result was a marriage of reasonable minds, and a large and harmonious family.

HE: It's a reasonable procedure
To advertise in The Argus,
It's a reasonable procedure
To make your requirements known.
When a gentleman feels alone
It's no business of nosey parkers
If the Classifieds of *The Argus*
Take a romantic tone.

It's a sane and humane procedure
To list particulars clearly,
It's a liberal fair procedure
To print your ideals in full.
Readers may think I'm a cool one
To publish rquirements, I'm merely
Stating particulars clearly,
It's a businessman's golden rule.

SHE: It's a modest and rational pastime
To read the Classifieid columns,
It's a chaste and literate pleasure
To note Mr Cole's address.
His earnestness must impress
And it lifted me out of my doldrums,
Reading his sensible columns,
To wish he should meet success.

	It's a prudent and practical venture
	To keep an appointment in person
HE:	Though an unforeseeable absence
	May cause a regrettable blush
SHE:	And blight the fair prospect of trust—but
THEY:	Should one care to repeat the excursion
SHE:	And keep the appointment in person
HE:	A merger can be discussed.

	It's a reasonable procedure
	To examine a partner's principle,
	It's mere commonsense to table
	Procedures, projections and stocks;
	It's nonsense to marry for looks—
BOTH:	Our amalgamation's invincible
	With a steady increase of principal
	And attention to balancing books!

Jones the Hangman

Jones the hangman is a lag
Jones the lag got lucky
Jones landed the hangman's job
Keeps him busy Mondays.

He's the one they scare the lads with
He's the artist with the cat,
He's the one lays on the lashes—
Jones, the keeper of the gallows!

Ties the neckties for the gentry—   *Jones does*
No-one finds the service lacking
In our model penitentiary—   *no-one!*
Turns all heads does Jones the hangman.

Now he's hanging of a woman   *hoo! a woman!*
She's a handful, she's a right'un,
Killing bubs, she got it coming,   *got it coming*
A bit if monstering, get her frightened.

Now they'll say as he's inhuman   *who? him!*
Now they'll tell him ladies like it,
Hangman's hands to slip the noose on   *see the hands*
Watch her swoon with the excitement.

Got a lay there, lady-friend, hey?   *hey hey*
Find out what the boy-friend handled—
Touch her up and feel her tremble,   *feel that*
None too fine for Jones the hangman.

Jones the woman-hangman, hang him!   *hang him*
Jones the hangman's cronies rag him
And you a man and hanging women!   *you a man?*
Says his wife to Jones the hangman.

Jones the hangman goes to prison
Week before he hangs the beauty
Got his bottle, won't go missing
Safe on hand to do his duty.

Jones the hangman's in his cell
But he won't hang no more,
Gone to hell is Jones the hangman,
That's what a razor's for.

The Lesson

A.S.A.L. parody night; in tribute to Gwen Harwood and Theodora Benson

Krötin has lost her middle C.
Click, click. Again to phone the tuner.
The student arriving right on three
attacks her *Giga* with a loony

breeziness, but disconcerted
by sudden gaps among the runs
and starved chords, when she's just got started
stops. Her teacher sighs, and stuns

the girl by insisting, "So—play on."
"It doesn't sound right." "Right it sounds
once in a century." When I'm gone,
she thinks, but genius on its rounds

will strike these faded roofs like bells
and drop a pianist here in Brisbane.
She'll be taught wrong, or marry, or else
turn to some halfway art like scribbling.

The student bags her music, scored
with 6B underlines. The exams
demand clean scores, so why does Frau
Krötin keep doing it? Krötin damns

that fresh face, rummages for gin.
Her own debut, the studio portrait,
white-armed and talented in Wien,
stays calm. Before the boy at four

Frau K sends off her future genius
to the backblocks, there to play along
at teachers' parties: *Bufo marinus*
ranging far inland from Toowong.

A Canberra Evening Muse

For A.D. Hope

Orpheus with his lute made trees
And the mountain-tops that freeze
Bow themselves when he did sing ...
  William Shakespeare, *Henry VIII*

Incorrectly operated, police radar could clock a tree at 68kph.
  Sydney Morning Herald 25.4.1987

I hear the Australian voice ... as if they were singing rather than
speaking, especially when they begin to recall events or things they
treasure.
  Sir Yehudi Menuhin

The young policeman spoke, his eyebrows weird
in the dashboard green, the busy figures blurred
on the radar dial as gums slipped by in the night:
Nothing at all on the road. It says sixty-eight!

Not them of course, hugging the legal limit
for once, and sober as pawnbrokers. Nothing in it,
a stroll of a reading anyway. Sydney-bound,
they made for bookings, and left bush roads behind.

Time wasted near Mullengandra on a girl
they found by the creek, had left them both perturbed.
A spirited thing, she would not know her place,
just liked it there, piss off, could get advice

from Someone At Canberra. No, she was not lost.
No wonder they didn't realise the trees they passed
were going their way—and the girl, gathering
the vastness of nature to her, shaping green

twigs for a wreath, beyond the straining fences
north-east, lifts over the silent Brindabellas
and heads for the reading. Putting down of fools
has made her late and careless—doctors on call

see past their lights a pregnant body star-
wise dissected, the unborn child fending the dark;
something has got to the horses where she shines,
and rutting stallions call great foaling on;

in the Batlow pub there's two men drowning glimpses—
one, Julia's backside; one, a detestable jilt
who'll be the death of a man yet. By the Lake they describe
a bleeding woman with candles, dressed like a bride.

She puffs up steps, the poetry-night attender,
flyer in one hand, ugg-boots for the weather.
Her Greek cheque awes the Door, reduced to books
(on sale) for change. The cheque will bounce. She takes

a nest-chair, settles her hams, breathes heavy, creaks,
gropes in her pockets, changes seat, repeats
the lot, recovers in convenient gloom.
A pause. Applause. The poet will resume—

she's missed the first half. Teacher-wise she listens,
then calms, then smiles. At last, at ease, uplifted,
transformed, by unpoetic eyes unseen,
she moves to pledge and crown him where he signs.

Alec! dear son! the trees attend; police
have clocked them; radar owns the Orphic race!
I hear the Australian voice; once more I learn
how myth and music shape our universe.

Dear love! for whom Andromeda consents
to be fine, since you said to, and the veiled gods and dead
poets prophesy new-tongued, now sing once more—
some young thing! Time it to your southern air!

Then, as our cops in terror ploughed a rout
of Goulburn gum-trees speeding—both sides—south,
the poet stood to his task, and remembered the day
he first went with reapers, a boy with his scythe to the hay.

Elizabeth and Red Socks in Perth

For Elizabeth Jolley

Elizabeth's wearing them. They go right up to her knee.
Wonderful! I say, in the voice of the energised house-guest,
but truthfully as it happens, truth in small things is a point with
    me,
I've been looking for long red socks. Right up to my knees.
Red Socks, writes Elizabeth. Shall go on looking.
In the little soft package, pink tissue, come two red socks
patterned with blue and black whirligigs, snug-topped, mid-calf.
I am sorry, Elizabeth sorrows, a prey to punctilio—
for tempered is the brief winter to the red-socked foot
with blue fleurettes. The morning and the evening, no contact—
a terrible force is unleashed, red socks in Perth
preen and tingle and nervously twiddle their price-tags,
they hang among offerings of half-hose and know they are chosen,
but only one pair may vie for the favoured right foot
and the very same pair for the left. The sports-shops do workouts,
there's straightening of hems at Aherns and bustle at Boans,
the little boutiques of the Stirling Highway bridle
We're nearest! and calculate tinkle and angle of doors
with trigonometrical precision, not lost on Elizabeth.
The pigeon-hole opens, delivering an office-issue envelope.
I am obsessed, red socks, she raves. *Please accept.*
And red they are, as hearts on Sicilian greeting-cards.
Elizabeth, I sigh in an art-hall of photographed buttocks,
Now I am hosed!—Not yet, she ventures, benevolence
scenting new samplings of socks, *I am not very good at it,*
knee-length is difficult. Meantime. These are nearer.
Home and half-hosed, blushing to the shameless ankles
in the light of Elizabeth's fiat, from shoe to shin

a Busselton sunset, secret Alpine festival
all the way from heel-bone to toe-tip and inside
the shin-slapping, seamy, but decent tube of the trouser,
I frisk in a vision of red socks, the world lisabelline
where red socks whirl in the sky to nest of an evening
and are found on the steps at breakfast, where handy house-
    husbands
cram them in vases, train them up trellises, serve
soufflé in a red-sock shell. Poor Honda, a red sock
I now see, and my once red room is a real grandma
of a red sock. Or is it the sock that's a shrunk red room?
Nothing so game in thought, on foot, in future
can be merely a remnant—it's tickly old Santa's scarlet
homing in on his solstice this month in Perth,
when raised from the mild blood-tempered bodysock sleep
I roll at the flame-knit foot of our great Player
round the day to red-socked Elizabeth's living-room fire.

The Champagne Launch of the Victorian Women Writers' Train, 1991

Out on the borders where road-markers are still saying Melbourne
to the astonishment of less clubbable States,
where the western district volcanoes rumble in their sleep of lava-
flows,
where the Tallest Tree in the World as viewed in atlases in
childhood
hides its imagined head from the loggers' survey-teams,
in farmland where a farmer with a yard of sixteen rusting Austins
kept for the parts
talks of getting the brother-in-law with his tractor to bury them,
in towns where Great Australian Readers breed the Great
Australian Writer,
where under the big river-gums a lone kid fishing and a lonely
inland cod
dream of the days of monster cod and schools of the monsters,
and elsewhere at dusk the tiger of Gariwerd gnaws
the ropes of the abseiler who hesitates,
and everyone wants to write about all that,

I see through the window of the Trains of the past and future
a figure on horseback who might be from the Snowy, or Joseph or
Ned or Hanrahan,
but not Mary, not yet a Dame, at Casterton, who would speak better,
though maybe it's Miles a little off track from Tilba Tilba or maybe
Eve,
saying:

> I went down to the station
> I'm accustomed to the row
> But you'll never in creation

Guess what trains are up to now—
You'll say imaginitis,
You'll say it's the champagne
There's a crew of women writers
Camped in every train!

And I reply:
They talk of the Orient Express
And trite funicular,
We have the Spirit of Progress—
We have the Norman Car!
In the conferential parlour
Where have parlayed the great,
We women go *en gala*
A-wording up our State.

And in the Mechanics' Institutes the oak tables straighten and the
    shelves
not yet yielded to the St Vincent de Paul and the Brotherhood
dream of translation to the new civic Library,
and heaters in halls and classroom projectors suffer power-surges,
and grown school-kids wonder if any of it will help with exams,
whatever acronym it is now, and the little ones wonder if they'll all
    be *old*,
and teachers give praise for the new squad briefly posted to the
    front line,
even if it interrupts the timetable—and also know they are
    friends—
and mysterious conjunctions prepare between that book and that
    child,
that writer and the work's true end, that listener and a phrase from
    the mouth of
that woman who sits hours listening, shaping what it is she hears,

until among starry word-traffic, ideas waving out of every window,
we might as well drink up and borrow a word from Galileo
for the Norman's Car world of words on wheels—and *it moves.*

Persons familiarly referred to in this poem are the Man From Snowy River, Joseph
Furphy, Ned Kelly, P.J. Hartigan ("John O'Brien")'s Hanrahan ("We'll all be
rooned"), Mary Gilmore, Miles Franklin and Eve Langley.

Arriving at Moongalba

Remembering Oodgeroo Noonuccal (1920–1993)

MEETING

I remember you, Kath, the quiet woman
sat with Kate on a bench at Manifolds':
our mandolines. Those Saturdays, the Wynnum
river-flats, a hawk circling, the ballads scored

for guitar, violin, recorder, lagerphone . . .
oh friends! Still lit and live, sixty years on!
John full-throated, haling the comrades in—
workers, students, blacks—but it wasn't your scene.

Just a few times I fronted your shy smile,
your frank laughter. Slim woman in a pleated skirt,
surely *Black Alice's* jolly sneers snagged your pride,
being bossed to play, even friendly bossing, stirred

a century's hurt. Your cause and your course clear
you were off through the weatherboard suburb to the bay
and out to the islands, your people waiting there
in want of words, you with the words to say.

NAMES

Amity

A ship under sail: a sighting—a sandy beach
offers its point to the neighbour island, offers
a watering place. A safe station, on the way
to the redoubtable mainland on the horizon
across the bay; the ship at anchor, meetings,
entry to the island's forest, its game, its people.
A fair prospect, needing a name: Amity?

A place apart, a site for quarantine.
Nearby, at Dunwich, shall be stalled and provisioned
society's refuse, leprous, drunken, delinquent.
As for the natives—supervision, a mission,
rations; benefits of civilisation—religion,
decency in dress, training for some kind of service.
And no-one should have to hear their benighted gibberish.

Oodgeroo
Mysteriously, the Noonuccal persevere.
Years of rules, prayer, lessons, labour—still
the children trap bandicoot, go crabbing, bring down birds
like the old folk time out of mind; the fishers of dugong
harvest the tides, scavenge timber cast up
in the mangroves—later, a crumbling slope of sand.
The bay swallows boats and kiosks, scours the shoreline.

Amity's heart beats on. After the War
the ferry's back to wake the bush retreat
of loners, misfits, missioners, handymen
and their women, making do, running the post,
the bakery, the new hall, the holiday cabins.
Improvising a community. Myora they call
the mission—but the blacks reach back to the real name—

and dads tell their kids the Indigenous creation,
the discipline of kinship with snake and curlew.
Language wears away but the names go on
and stories nest in the people. In city offices
there are children who've run from Bunyip in the dark,
who know a great love clothed the silky oak.
Whose mission names hardly fit. Like young Kath.

After the freedom buses, the referendum,
after the first Indigenous seisin of land,
after the years as maid, stenographer,
after the poems critics called "naïve",
"uneducated"—wisdom they'd no ears for—
the girl named for paperbark crosses the bay,
returns to kin and country. Claims her name.

Moongalba
Place holds the people. They wander—place is inside them,
staking its claims, reserving its treasures. What place?
Maybe the space by a mother, between her bed
and the wall. Or backyards of a childhood. Maybe an endless
plain with its secrets for living. For Oodgeroo,
 the green island in the sea's embrace, Mudjerribah
miscalled Stradbroke. The grove Moongalba, miscalled
Myora for the decades of a colonial season.
Mother, worker, activist, time remakes her,
elder and teacher in the Sitting Down Place, Moongalba.

The claims of place: find me, recover the old ways.
In the finding, the gift: generations, voices longed for,
paths of old retraced, surprising radiance
of then-new skies. The girl named for paperbark
outlives the cities and honours, outlives anger.
Her work, words that outlive even injustice.
Oodgeroo gathers lore from the bush thickets,
from the tellers of tales, from a childhood remembered.
At the Sitting Down Place she rears tree-trunks
figured with carpet-snake, her father's clan;
builds a Round House, shelter of welcome,
a place offered and received. Here children sit,
a ferry-trip from home. And tourists, wondering.

The gift of place is set out, food of life: landscape
the city supplanted, laws of the land before streets,
greetings at the gathering of peoples.

And tales, truths:
Tell them of brown kids picked on
Tell them of confidence gone
Of lives and language taken
Of anger awakened

But, more,
To care for creatures of foot fin and wing
Cherish the bush that greens our wandering
Together no matter the colour of the face
make of our meetings a special place: Moongalba.

FROM THE OTHER SIDE

The dead do not stay dead. There's your Dad
teaching kids still in the voice of Oodgeroo;
for punishment, putting the kids on cut and dried
mission rations—that's unsurprising news
of the habit of white contempt, from the other side.

On both sides of the Bay kids were empire-bred,
saluted and sang God Save and marched into school.
Foreigners, natives—suburban talk assured
us they weren't much good, were placed on earth to be ruled
by us, who knew nothing of you. On the other side.

But you, Oodgeroo, you refused to be nullified.
You heard the put-downs, you saw what a sneer could do.
You mourned what was going, you spoke of making new.
You stood on your land with the lore you lived as proof
of title, you asked us across, to sit side by side.

THE DARK CLEARING

Here is the shady clearing
of honour and farewell,
here the Noonuccal, neighbours,
and visitors off the ferry.
Here the piling of branches
long home for her large life
hailed now a hero.
Funeral games are on promise:
the sorry pronouncements,
the treaty, true amity,
the intermingling.
Here is the woman abased
who spoke from a high place
found words against hate,
who denying suspicion
and separation
harboured laws for living.
Curlew, cousin, have you called
the three nights' warning?
Yet this is no death—

Flowers are scattered
words uttered
the body passes.
Poet and teacher
her place murmurs of her
in sea-winds, the surf
mounting the beaches
down to the dire rip
of Jumpinpin.
The leaf-thick paths
the shadowy glade

the glancing lights
of bark-shedding bush
are the smile of the girl
named for paperbark,
who saw beyond the going
to the growing back
to amity achieved
always the people meeting
at the Round House
at the Sitting Down Place
Moongalba.

Celebrations

Writing Cards

This too is a season.
Each year's slowing
brings hailing of friends—
piling of cards,
addressing of envelopes,
panic of posting-dates.

This is my motorcade, friends,
passing your gateway,
ambushing your route.
You can take in my broadcast
of personalised sentiments,
cursory or the full letter-scene.
Accept the giveaway life-video
edited with you in mind.

At the end of the nostalgia
in they fly, card-hordes
crowding the new year!
You I have known,
your old-new voices
talk half-recalled *us*
towards *you* half-recognised.
I update my records
and question the ravelling
ways and way-stations:
fifty friends bound to their journeys,
fifty strangers entered in my heart.

Where did you come from?
How did you gather?
What brings you to my line of journey
and me to yours?

How did you slip through my hands?

Page from a Sketch-Book, Ballad Night 1959

In memory of Kate Manifold, d. 1979

Serpent, mandora and guitar
hang on their loops and nails between
the hour achieved and the hour
of taking down again:
>   still before sounding.

Tuning her mandoline, she leans
intent to fix the recorder's A.
Fingers listen, silence
ripples her skirt in graces
>   still before sounding.

See where her profile lifts, alert,
poised in life's full tide. That calm
searched out the humble and hurt
like a remembered song
>   still before sounding.

Who played ballads there that night?
and stroked the cats, and carried tea?
roaring the Bandicoots'
refrains, with John's hearty
>   bellow resounding!

The man's part and the tender answer,
who could doubt they sang themselves,
John's Willy to Kate's Nancy!

Then whooped through free-for-alls
　　　　　wildly resounding!

Knowing her young, cat-lithe and wild,
so much fine laughter in her face,
he must have known what steel
held our rich common bass
　　　　　still sounding.

Word from the desolate music-room:
she falters and her song is pain.
Her cheer strikes grieving dumb
and every note to stone
　　　　　unresounding

till we hear, and thank our loss, and beyond
find her, the harmony that's in
new song and new-found friend.
Hang up her mandoline.

Venetia

Venetia, who with perfect courage let me paint
her London ceiling with violent unshiftable Dulux
(a case of only my boredom with well-sized plaster)
and with perfect sang-froid viewed the botch. And yet
that summer made rendezvous in Istanbul
to hitch to Beirut. Beside her on the quay, surprise,
our third—a monster case., a chair-sized amphora. So
it was trucks we hitched, shuddering, radiator hissing,
to Ankara, and onward and over Taurus.
The Syrians had a coup d'état—by luck we didn't
stay in Latakia. Borders shut behind us. We made it
with the gift-crock, in time to be flown to a Melbourne wedding
whose children are grandparents now, the urn—in whose hall?
And Venetia—that ceiling!—that was the last I saw of you.

Approaching Jean Rhys' *Wide Sargasso Sea*

Dominica, 1962

Cocking a massive chin
Doctor Elisabeth Müller,
met who remembers how
at wooden Roseau decimated
by the last great fire,
takes me in.

It's been days
watching dominoes played
WI style to a fanatic
scrum on deck . . . the Island-hopping
green and peeling *Island Palm*
drops you ashore, to wash up
at her whitewashed room.

How you work at travel!
A pudgy girl come from study
to help a "developing country"
you long to understand
place, patois, politics
and snap in magical colour
orange plaster on shops,
head-scarves and bare feet. Instead
you have the large Frau Doctor's
jailing under Hitler, told
over pots of seedlings and bouillabaisse
under the bland blue noon.
Not easy to dispose of the Frau Doctor's
books and confidences,
heavily breathing the blue air.

Nor her jail-visiting nor
hand-towels hemstitched by prisoners
nor her Wordsworthian crush
on the waterfalls of the interior—
innocence and youth restored,
her heart leaping up when she beholds, etcetera,
along forest paths, etcetera,
there isn't time to show.
You can't believe it in a woman
of her age and size.

The poem moves sideways
on a large woman's literary passion:
our novelist—did you know?

Twenty-five years silent
befuddled in icy England
Jean Rhys is telling it all:
the long-dead Creole
girls going down to bathe
demure in concealment,
each a bedevilled secret
path to the interior.

Well: Doctor Elisabeth
shows you the convent.
Creole twice over
from Australia and this posting
you understand nothing.

You have to wait for the book,
Elisabeth's gift when it comes.

Jean Rhys's *Wide Sargasso Sea* was published in 1966, 27 years after the last of her
previous novels.

The Cold

For Barbara Giles

You say there is a cold place in me.
Over the day's first coffee
with a bar of heat in the kitchen,
over books, round mementoes
it's there. Blue graph like a nipple.

And you laughed like a girl
in among your poems
and the women and children your sons brought.
Your cushions jostled and your bread warmed.
Your backyard crawled with leaf,
the reaching towering vine.
When it's cut back you find pegs,
the lost tea-towel, neighbours.

Your poems, getting it all in:
sharp on a word, the touch tender,
bold as principles and homage.
Your eyes unpaired for colour,
the weave and bossed jewel of Celtic make—
sky-web of light, earth-bowl of shade.
The goddess's odd hands.

The nose-in kerb, walkover gate.
Flowerpots. The belled greeting.
Skewed in its perch on books
behind the opening door
an anatomical hand curves ready to hold,
models skin, blood-branching, tendons,

lifts away the layers to bone.
The blue-flowered china cat
nuzzles, now, the ghost of little Blackie,
guest of 'eighty-five,

when snug in your back-room a season
I traced the streets of Roman London
late, by a baseless lamp
condemned not to sit or stand.
I aimed its blackbonnet glare,
lay warm, went on reading.
You prowled the house at night
like-minded, devoured paper.
In your brick gate-post's hollow
—the letter-box, mortared, clammy—
snails moved in and set to,
shredding your steady mail
to colour their journeys.

Leaving or staying: cold
for my grandmother, doubting her choices—
her children brought up abroad
awry, breaking the pattern,
at home in an unread pattern;
for Mum, the company wife
through half a dozen transfers—
strong on tact and economies,
growing away from friends,
mounting judgment, stifling
news of herself young, her sisters.

Nineteen-eighty, you visited
rounding Arthur's corner-shop

to my home, home I headed,
home of children and stories,
home of the dog and my young trees
the silly buyer cleared.
On bushfire days we languished in the long room
or by the lime-tree—light and thorns.
The dog crawled under the house
to doze at the dugs of shade
or lay on the kitchen vinyl,
always the same spot.
I came in barefoot. I lay down.
In a room innocent of ash,
the cold place. Breath from before us.
The house whispered its muffled things.

If you want my fire
stand on my hearthstone.

Bereavement

In memory of Rosemary Wighton

What am I to do? You suffer, our friend will die,
friends phone and say, in their own way, she's dying.
Pat gives the number. Sometimes they put you through.
Nin says she won't be going home. You suffer.
You plan to fly, reap a last understanding,
bestow . . . but can't you tell she's out too far,
her kind don't signal. Steer how you will, she's on
ahead, her dead have come to meet her, you
will have to wait for your own twilight passage.
Years to recall the welcome of her garden,
the paved walled yard, the herbs, a bench with cushions,
books, family snaps mosaic'd on a board,
her final task—editing her father's memoir.
The upright smiling woman hiding pain.

The Year

In memory of Lauris Edmond

One year on, dear Lauris,
from our last exchange of cards
I write, and send the glorious
bird in a spray of luminous watercolour.

The reply's in time for Christmas.
Out falls my peacock card
from the envelope, and alas,
unlooked-for words: a daughter's news of your death

almost a year past. You were gone
whenever I thought of you, then—
remembering our night of New Zealand's triumphant election,

enjoying how we'd talk of Clark
and your GG and head judge, all women.
Suddenly gone, on a sunny Friday morning.

But for me, all along you'd been there,
your live glance and crinkling smile
and your once-red turbulent hair
and your passionate commitment. Not dead, but planning to visit—

and you stayed till the second card struck
its mournful note, its waterbird
in the wetlands' undulant dark
calling the end of that year's mysterious life.

Answering Doris

When I die, I want to be an ordinary memory.
   – from 'When the fat lady sings' by Doris Leadbetter

Sorry, Doris. Words pollies can't manage even for murder,
occur to me, reading your all-too-impossible order.

Your Mrs Craven's* métier was losing her head
to sustain a leading role in the Book of the Dead,

going on to rendezvous—sans froid, sans panic—
with her metaphoric selves on the Titanic

while splendidly leaving her father in heaven uninformed
(If he wants me, somebody will tell him where I am)—

Well!

He *could* find you, Doris, gazing a sense of adventure
and wit and flair on poets at the Writers' Centre.

Or updated, throned in the company of books
and Kris and Retta at Collected Works.**

But Doris, wherever you are, the party's there
and when the last word's said, you leave us here

a memory dear
and extraordinaire.

*Mrs Arthur P. Craven, widely-travelled heroine of poems by Doris Leadbetter.
**A fine portrait of Doris somehow moved from the wall of the Writers' Centre to
preside in the bookshop's busy portrait corner.

It's Not Right

In memory of Lisa Bellear

aunty-caller
kicker-up of twisters
sweet urban bird
day never drowned out your voice
how come you shifted to night
like town sparrows long after dusk
      it's not right

    mickey-taker
    strong shoulder
    living on dares
fire at the heart of change
how come you ran out of heat
run off your feet in the straight
      it's not right

    winning card
    woman of words
    welcomer
    making waves
    wowing our legions
all of us rocked in your wake
and girl, how you sparked with the barrackers
how does mere flesh make apologies
Lisa, glad warrior, for taking the fight
out of life, out of the light?
      it's not right.

Two for Joyce Lee at Ninety

NINETY! LOVELY NUMBER!
Many of us at ninety will add three.
Some of us at ninety will say eighty-five.
Most players still standing
will tolerate guesses down to seventy
and as high as the sky,

while the rest of us, unaware,
fertilising austral plantings,
will no longer be teasers of wind
or items in the literary calendar.

But there are those who lengthen their stride.
Ninety—no trouble at all,
simply a figure to juggle with,
time to laugh in the sun.

HEAVEN
Heaven is here and now.
If anyone says
no wheelchairs in heaven
no knees or hips in heaven
no white hair and no thinning skin—
I see what they mean,
but really, they want to be dead.

Heaven is here and now
with language growing all round—
weeds of it bold and tall
jostle for the ball

in wordy arenas,
and tended gardens
break out in favourite fruit
where poets of ninety, still writing
mulch their much living—
each memory puts out a shoot,
the new lyric sprouts and we savour
scents of the herb-pot
one heavenly day in spring.

To Say the Least

Canadian Poets from A to Z, *edited and introduced by P.K. Page*

Dear P.K., when I understand
it's you I read in the pages
of your anthology—you
loving the singularity
of each tiny poem—you savouring
devising their delicate array—

I remember the day
I met you at the launch of the children's book
at a Victoria BC bookseller's,
tall and fine among ordinary mortals
(dear P.K.—not of course gone
while memory's in play),

and embrace the hope again
to be read in my works large and small
and also where self offers—
ushering forward
best friends and words treasured—
to say the least.

Peter's Dream

In memory of photojournalist Peter Davis, who quoted Ilan Ramon,
an astronaut on doomed space-shuttle Columbia: "Today was the first
day that I felt that I am truly living in space. I have become a man
who lives and works in space."

Now your photographs dance in our lives, your avatars!
a gust of greeting, views from the unfinished journey.
One twirls with a poem, a binary: seen and said,
said and seen. Not a remove—a partnership.
Fainter are your dreams, whose print refuses to be read,
so bright is the light of today's going on without you,
so ruthless. But a rousing at your name, your spirits, your book
rescued from the dark—how everything loved can be recovered.
Memory: your hillside work-room, all India; the puns,
the roll of your head in a Tamil "I'm listening" mode.
You award us this musing: the European Union, no less,
commissions you to write for the world of a space project,
one more, one infinite window. Now with Ilan Ramon
you have become a man who lives and works in space.

Hazel

In memory of Hazel Rowley, biographer

Light in motion. A blade
swung joyously in battle, as when
to a startled Faculty, she blazed
contempt on a mediocre Dean.
Too good a scholar to keep tapping
at the last prescribed for academic
footwork, too various, too rapid
to repeat for years set lectures.

Full-fledged, her flights abroad
pursued mastery she admired,
heroes of free thought, the word,
enlightened power. But the dark
fell on her shining, as she fired
anew. And the embers ache.

Paul Sherman

The golden boy is making his stage-right entrance
elsewhere. How after sixty years, with his fate
upon him, is he still the clear-profiled director
of our student *Coriolanus*—a hundred stages
ahead of him, children in a hundred schools
ripe to be held, cajoled by the antic craft,
all those people to inhabit, the blaze, the foolery,
the words, the passions speeding, all brakes off?

A life of impersonations, exit leaving
the *Melba* play, poems, and by time's grace
friendship re-lit, long talk, the bolognaise
I won't forget, recall of Eunice being
a corpse, teaching our cast to roll down stairs
hurtless, to cheers . . . curtain for a final scene.

Paul Sherman was a fellow-student of mine at the University of Queensland.
A teacher, actor, director, and later dramatist and poet, he toured extensively,
presenting literature in Queensland schools — mostly one-man performances of
Shakespeare.

The Reading
In memory of Shanti Devadasan

Never got to her grave on Quibble Island,
somehow a comment on the mess of it all,
somehow laughter from beyond.

Shanti, my dear Cesario, Viola in sari,
I your Olivia send by this a ring
of grieving thought, of memories: no more reading
Shakespeare in the Chennai mall, the silk-shop—
regions Shakespeare never knew, but given
a century, only a century, who knows?
Headed east by the Serenissima—
Philippi—Actium—the Nile, our Will
was ripening toward the Mahabharata,
the gallant tales, the gold-skinned delicate-
fingered dancing god and cow-eyed girls
and partnership in a Bollywood studio.

No more dreams of escaping the public service,
no more meals in your stifling concrete flat,
no more mother-joy in a masterful daughter
moving into film, rambunctious Rashmi.

Unfair! that a departmental head who tries
to prevent appointment by nudge and who-you-know,
who juggles or chokes on, sorting somehow through
thousands and more thousand applications
for one menial position, takes infection
untimely, sinks in hospital, comes to wreck
at surely not yet fifty, almost before

I'm off the plane home I had to board,
leaving you bedded among the river mud-flats
of holy Adyar, a lass unparalleled.

Guttering years cannot blur or stow in the dark
that reading. Teachers after Chennai classes
turning pages in Illyria, lady,
among bolts of silk, unroll the beloved
fable of finding the lost, joining the sundered,
conquering time's atrocities, contraries meeting
in sacred joy. Back to a man at his metrics
in a cramped room, restoring to life a son
twinned to a radiant and living daughter,
their youth, their play replayed, mimic salvation
by love, by inspired trickery, by anything. By words.

Last nearing—hope on hold—flickers—the vigil
parked between hospital blocks while a friend enquires.
Rats in the alley's litter, their domain.
Not much in the way of light. And later visits—
asking and telling, laughter, a play to devise,
all of it—flares doused in the narrowing chute.

What words for the woman, dead? "Her state is well"?
"Leading those graces to the grave"—what solace?
Charmers juggle with death. Fold them in tides
down by the river-mouth, start at their glittering motes
upstream at dusk. Lose them again to the main.

And Quibble Island—what would its scrubby shores
and cemetery paths solve of the endless puzzle?
Shanti lies down. We all lie down. And glances
shine beside a wall, then slip behind.

Screens multiply. Shanti, our hour remains
present and dear. Out of time, in mind.

"A lass unparalleled", "Illyria, lady", and the quoted phrases are from Shakespeare's *Twelfth Night*.

Shakespeare's eleven-year-old son Hamnet, twin to Judith, died in 1596, about five years before the writing of *Twelfth Night*. The play is about twins, parted by a shipwreck, who think one another dead but to everyone's surprise are reunited, each having found love.

Near and Dear

Matters

They take the house
fifty-fifty.
He does instalments.
She pays health-care.
I'm telling you
things that don't matter.

He pays the power.
He phones.
She phones.
He pays. She squirms.
I'm telling you
incidentals.

He struts. She shrugs.
He cooks. She sours.
Whoever shuts
a door, they suffer.
I'm telling you
one scenario.

She concentrates.
He avoids. She mutters.
He waits. She fusses.
They drive, out loud.
I'm telling you
another script.

She views. He mows.
She rakes. They edge.

They weed. They pile.
They plan. They plant.
They water. They agree.
They chat and saunter.

Things that matter
have just caught up.

The Score

My tiny thoughts
are second-rate
he reads his watch
I'm always late
I ride the clutch
I spoil the kids
I clean too much
I always did
can't cook for nuts
can't dress can't save
can't give the love
his mother gave
my friends a laugh
my work a sham
I've got no sense
but I've got him.
How brave I am!

Couple

She wrestles with sealed plastic.
How, she grates, do little old ladies ... ?
They don't, he comes in on cue
with erect gaze eyeing
the middle of her head as probably
a blur. They're found days afterwards
with all the things around them
tied up, screwed shut, sealed tight.
Right, right. Both of them wait.
And the little old gentlemen, of course,
died years before, trying
to make do on catfood. She applies this
as intended. He's seeing the therapist.
She was only after the sliced cheese.

Angry Woman

An 84-year-old Japanese woman has let her hair grow more than three metres long after a fight with her husband 28 years ago. —
Newspaper item

HUSBAND
All my wanderings ago, I started
swimming towards you in the night.
Now our grandson is a man.

I pillowed my young head on your blackness.
At the touch of tide I forgot
beginnings and endings.

Red dawn sprang, wrack and then
rain till the end of the world.
The runnels thickened,

breakers mounted, the tempest of you
wakened and spread. You swore
I would never see daylight.

Behind me is twice the life of a man
and still I am swimming towards you
in these grey waters.

WIFE
First joining is easiest.
I remember our meeting, warm as night-wind
off the river-lands—

through vine-thickets, cabbage-palms, air
of cedar and plantain, pineapple and chilimoya.
Mornings were sultry,

water swirled heavy with sand
out from the river-mouth, the gem-pebbles sank
in mud and shell-grit

rolled by the salt swell.
The sea glinted with fish-heads, sky closed
torn with lightning—

I am trapped in my promise to myself.
It is late in the world and elements I mixed
fling down plantations.

The Life Inside

A little house, a little house.
Heard from the yard:
fresh voices at the door.
A little house.

A little house.
The shelves that fill,
and cups along the board.

A little house.
Two chairs pushed close,
the crossword page filled out.

A little house.
Heard from the bed:
the hot wind all night long.

A little house.
The photos stare.
The phone shrills once and stops.

A little house.
Heard by no ear
the messages repeat.
A little house.

Reproach

"I've never changed." Your problem, friend,
though I can't say I'm not pained.
Regret? No, that nudges up to blame.

Constancy. What's the use, what price
lies decades old—that curse
we needn't carry on. What worlds

we've lived since our uncertain dallying
(your hand on my arm, pressed oddly).
Both of us led ploys we couldn't follow,

the closeness jarred. Still we write cards,
replay the mistaken sharing
of times when we so truly cared.

Unsuitable Friendships

In memory of Rex Cramphorne

What can be done about 'unsuitable friendships'
thirty years on, except to bray for as long
as monumental bronze that none of them then
killed, louder than Patriot-fended explosions
of the Mother of all Wars, that none of them killed?
Demolished or repainted or unshelved?—
I ask—my cupboard where you set up house
with books and discs, despite your bitter mother
phoning the Department that could have ended
a career I found thirty later ways to wreck,
but lobbed me on my way despite your mother
to land in Cambridge's last colonial shower
still whole in folly, on course for Oslo, Damascus,
die romantische Strasse, more unsuitable friendships.

The Drama Director Practises Exit

In memory of Ken C-D.

Meeting at Myers. Time for a leak, he said,
wilting over the counter. Nobody's fooled.
Over tea, it's new money arrangements, foiled
the Bank, paying a few debts on the side.
Perhaps less time on the counter, it's absurd
he's not directing, heaven knows why he's failed
to get a lectureship, the jobs are filled
by academics—in Drama! They should be sued.

As of now, he has kitchen work, three nights—it's money.
Perfumes—he's permanent, as long as he can take it.
Transfusions keep him going, more study, he
enjoys the tutes. He'll read his novel to as many
friends as can come, the twenty-eighth. A ticket
to Wagner. A grant next year. Who's fooling who?

The Vigil

You smell out Charon. Stench of waterweed
and stagnant bilge. The dusk laden with rumour
from the countless poled crossings. Regret and dread.
The beckoning shadow, the boatman's hooded scrutiny.
So here you hover, peering through the blinds—
a kid on a date—for the classical walk to the ferry.
And gawk as this gigolo, bad teeth and painted grin,
struts up to a neighbour door, hales the unwary
fool from behind it. It's *him*. He stood you up!
There they go, joining the night-world—down to the jetty,
lip to lip, arm in arm, off to their games.
Yours is the lot to follow with hobbled step
or sit and peer as the ferryman's manifest
turns page after page. But not to read the names.

Mother-in-law

Becoming a mother-in-law,
to put on all at once the halo
of a Queen Mother flower-border hat,
a competitive smile and deferential
back-seat tastes in music;
learning to be a mother-in-law, with
foreground   a pot-plant,
backcloth   decorum,
framed expressions of individuality
and one doorway of unflappable greeting;
at last the mother-in-law scores
a daughter's startled appreciation
of parental tales of courtship,
and this without even once again
saying I do!
      And mothers-in-law
(their generation claiming them at last)
themselves have a few surprises coming:
the fine mien of the father of the bride,
a renewed interest in tableware
and tolerance, even welcome
for the new nickname on the old daughter—
the name she'll answer to and go by
and grow into or grow out of love with
and live wearing;
      while the mother-in-law
brings in her arms at each visit
wrapped like a sweet-smelling garment
not unparceled lightly
what a daughter's children may find

one day, and screw up their eyes
to follow its incredible stitching:
a hand-worked childhood, played in
and washed and ironed and folded
between them.

Daughters

"A coven of witches:" I say of them, "brutes"—
and I mean that the weight
of that self you keep, studiedly,
using phrases like "personal space",
from outsiders,

they throw at me
frankly as leaves in a gale
and heavy as boots,
and laugh in cahoots, the tribe of them
harrying, having a go at me;

they're my insiders,
the ones who know what I mean
by cleaning, or silence,
leaning, half-listening each to the other,
delight

and commotion
as we swoop in our moment of life—
I hazard, they hazard—
unfurling between us the note
of our incantation.

Sayings of My Mother

1930
They've let the blinds down, a brazen afternoon,
rattle of slats, dot-dash sun-spots on the boards.
Over shandies, the girls have got out the mah-jong
from the dresser drawer, they're tangled up in flowers and winds.

The English salesman roped in on his weekend breather
from selling vacuum-cleaners at Leonora
puzzles, takes a dash at it, making the party go.
The quiet girl comes out from talking with Iris—

she is about to surprise herself—and bends
her bobbed head to study the pieces. Out of the blue
(retort to his tennis-court volleys) she taps his shoulder.
"You don't want to play that silly game!"
So hands are re-dealt, patterns whisked into change,
the new world essayed. And no revokes.

2008
Now to the albums. We've tried blowing up the photos.
The screen can take them in to a dust-storm of dots
and out past the eye-pitched view. Adjust, adjust—
suddenly posed by the bus at the tourist-lodge

there they are, she peers, she recognizes
two elderly figures. Something in the stance. We've done it!
She's leaning through years, tapping the dark glass
like startled moths: "Come back! Let's have some fun!"

Decades crumple to a night in the zippy thirties:
off the road and over the small-scrub plain
skitters his Willis, jibbing at burrows and tussocks,
headlights jumping, hoyed rocks, rabbits playing games.
All the lighting we can manage won't hold the image
galvanic, the freckled print, a blur, Dad's face.

THE SISTERS
Seventy-five years on, blind, sitting in her kitchen
the bright young thing is cajoled to speak of her dead
sisters. They all married out. Their mother died young
between the first defection and the next.

The heel-tapping eldest—the charmer!—it was broke faith,
though the killer was a faulty mitral valve.
The next, brooding and shy, a canny bidder,
rounded a gentile life with jewish rites.

My atheist mother's questioning her fast-fixed
past the beloved mother didn't have to face:
and had she lived? "It would have broken her heart.
I never would have been brave enough." Aghast
I scan the tides, the rock-passage navigated,
the chasm, the narrows, the odds I slipped through, me.

Safe

My mother is crouching at the back of her mind.
She has not many ideas to go on.
Her interests have faded. Her sisters are gone.
It is long since she securely recognised
the daily carers, daughter and grand-daughter.

She rouses to rummage the cupboards—all hers—
for anything to do,
snatches a cleaning-rag, sticky tape, cards she can't read.
Asked, she says she wants scissors.
Asked why, she does not stay to answer.

Wakeful, she has left her walking-frame.
Tape tangles her fingers.
It is four-thirty in the night and nothing,
nothing in her indomitable body or her own warm home
will be allowed to kill her.

The Dream

I watched above the bed in which I lay.
And on a bed, sheeted, my mother, dead
ten months now, stirred. But she is gone, I said,
and saying it returned still mired in care
to where my mother stilled with barely a word
left from the hundred years she sealed away.

O strange arrival, seeing death reversed,
the sheet tensing with movement, the unspoken
demand we resume together, she being wakened.
A wondering horror held me, and her hair
as never in life, was mine, and I lay there
creature of her imagining, as at first.

Dad

I live inside my father's
feet, hands, eyes,
and allergies. My nose drips
and I remember Dad,
obstinately mowing and weeding
in an age innocent of Zyrtec.

I knew my father young,
in his thirties. No other child
or grandchild was thrown up and caught,
passed snaky round his torso
and over his shoulder. Who else
was skipped a whole city block
fast, with tremendous strides,
fearful exhilaration!
I was Diddles and later Girlie,
Barry was Blue. The nicknaming
goes on, incurable, genetic.

When Dad learned cabinet-making—
a demobilisation choice—
I stood at the bench and thrilled
(holding hard where I was told)
at the mighty planing of planks,
the tightness of mortice and tenon.
I turned the grindstone, sparks
flew from the chisel. The smell
of good wood, maple, with me
till I inherited the desk—
its drawers still running like silk,

his original french polish
dishonoured with estapol
to match dark-stained deal.
Now, back to its honeyed grain.

Dad, you couldn't know
I would have the wrecked drawers
of the school-desk you made me, remade—
cleaned, squared, repainted
for second life. And the silver
presentation pieces
picked over, packed off to grandchildren
some of whom won't care:
candlesticks, trays, the water-jug,
sideboard flower-bowl ("the Davis Cup").
But I have the desk-elephant,
the penstand, the useless plaque,
the tiny trophy-cup—curios
of my childhood. Dad, your career.

At 99, frail, frustrated—
me off teaching in India—
you told my kids how clever
I'd been, a 'natural'. Like Grannie,
your school-results framed and hung.
Dad, I weep at your pride.
How dear a tale. But me away, you died.

Died understood. I took
all you gave, the faith in family,
the English cousins, brothers
you hardly saw in the staggered
boarding at school—your regret

a late pious guilt. You'd said
their doors would be open: they were.
Farmers, technicians, in banks,
a rugby selector; one poet.
Back to the man you trained for,
showing Mr Hare's draught-horses,
colossal Shires, manes plaited.
Rumours of why you left:
Hare's tennis-playing daughter, dead now,
cannot explain or demur.
Your mother, garnering your visits,
kept the dickey door-handle
as you left it, half-repaired, waiting.
Fifty years: the weekly letters
her assurance, your atonement.

Things forgotten, half-known, treasured.
Their life, my hands, your gift.

Afterward

Dad, you ran out on me. Third time
I was gone for too long. Twice
I said "Be here when I get back".
Third time I said nothing. You were tired,
sick of living in a chair,
sick of carers, readmission
to the Cabrini. And thinking back,
back to the brothers you hadn't
known between school and the colonies.

The funeral amazed us all.
I couldn't stop smiling.
The business colleagues came,
a generation younger than yours,
known from dinners, and retired.
All of them, as it happened, smiling.
The neighbour with the accent
Mum couldn't stand; she smiled too.
The cousin whom you fathered
for three years, way back when;
he spoke of you with love
I sparked to recognize
and all of us smiled, confident
in each other's eyes; we all knew why.
I felt you everywhere, a good man
in his place, who'd got it right
most of his life. The one who cried
was the one who'd never known you.

Mum sat between grandchildren.
Seventy years, laid away.
Three weeks later, on the grass
grown where you raised tomatoes
with love, we spread ashes. With love.

Cordelia's Music for Lear

If I tell you your liegemen wait
and your monster horse
you peer through the crazed hedge
show off bird-tufts
and paste them with licky
to a horse-skull melting like candy.
You have to laugh.

Come from the twigs, summon
the lineage of straw
colouring-in our blood
to daub your scratches.
Father, I gather
your warrior-hand all bone
in my hands' bowl,

in my shawl, in my hair's shade.
My young esquires
paint birds upon their shields,
each golden eye
and rainy bird-voice
a washed soul beginning.
Lie soft, be called.

www.ingramcontent.com/pod-product-compliance
Lightning Source LLC
Chambersburg PA
CBHW030939090426
42737CB00007B/479